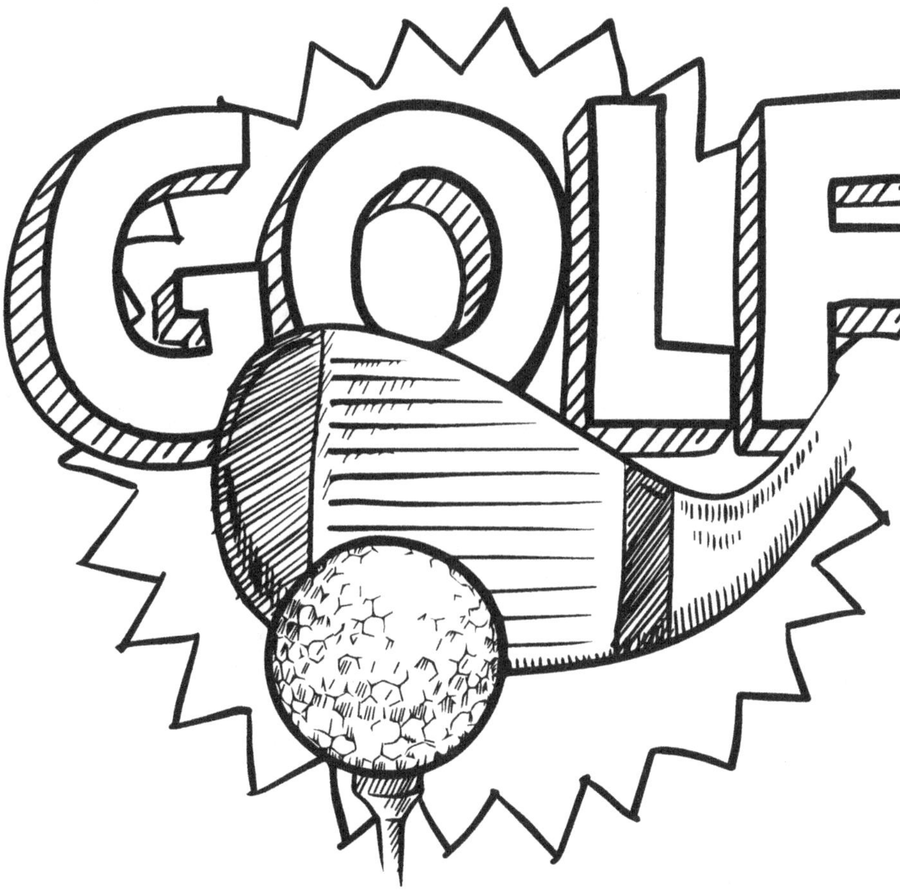

THIS BOOK BELONGS TO

....

....

....

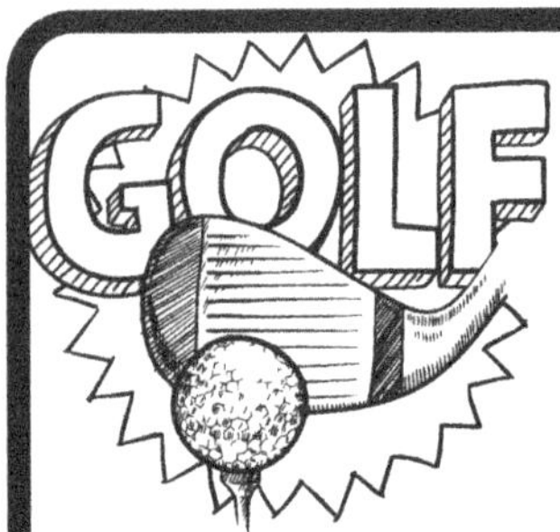

COLOR TEST

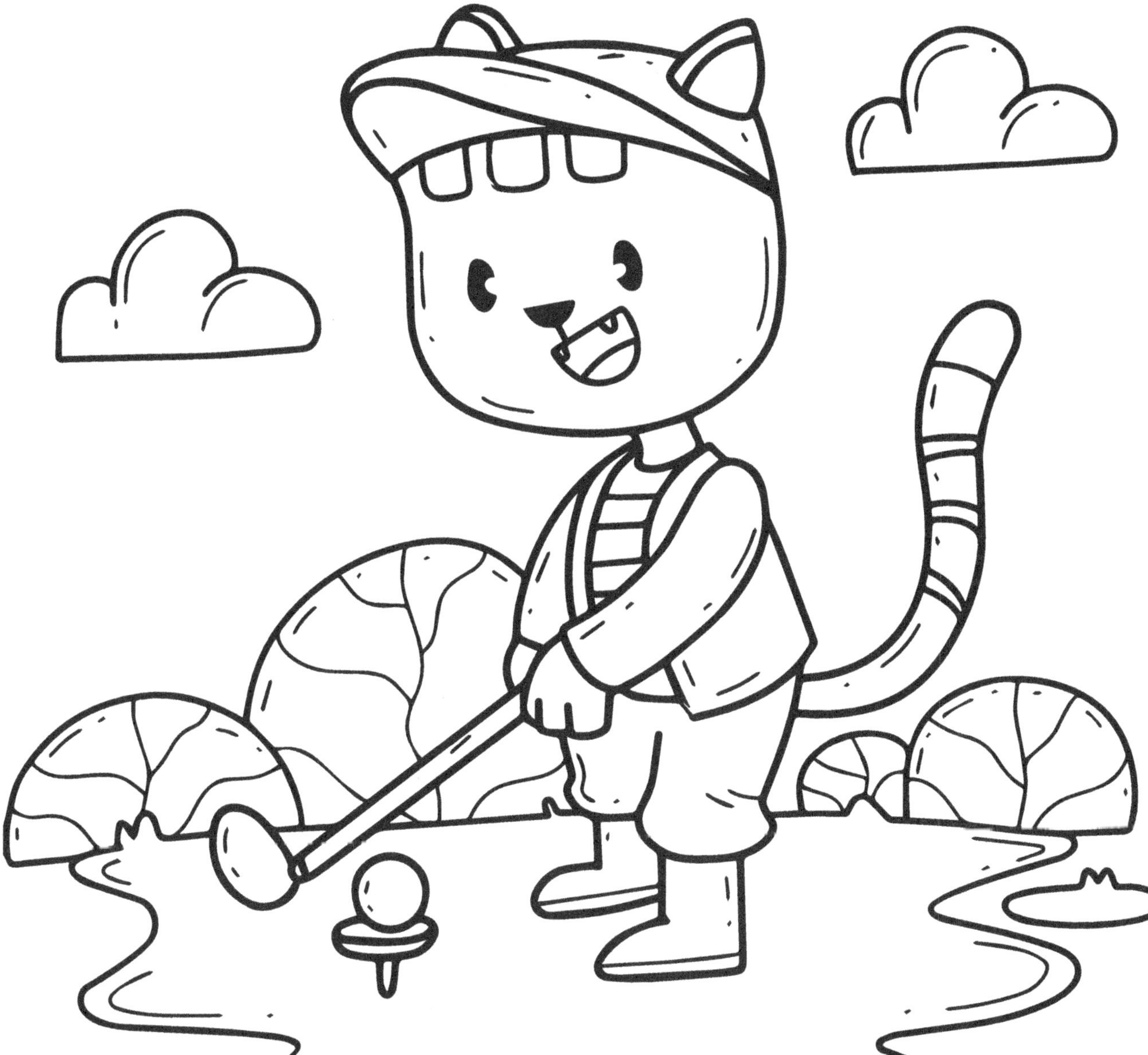

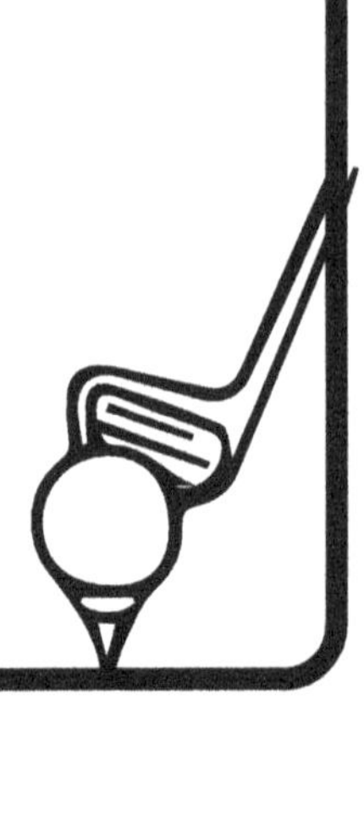

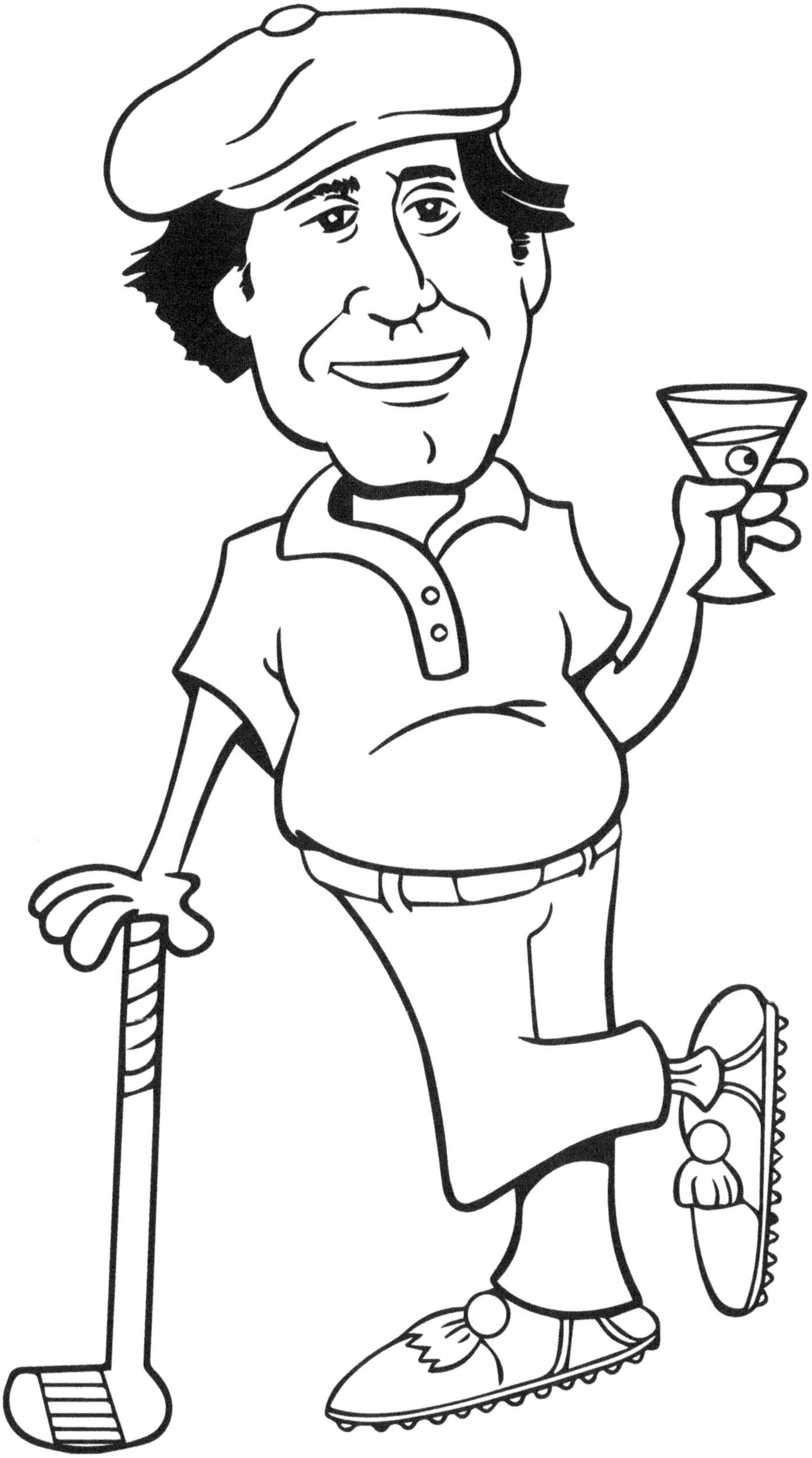

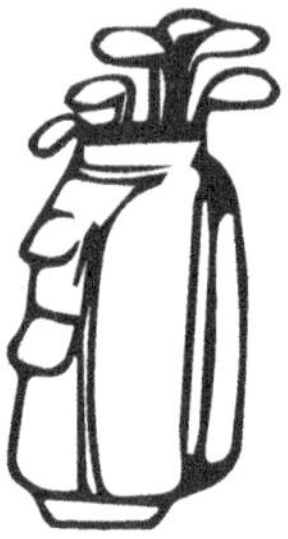

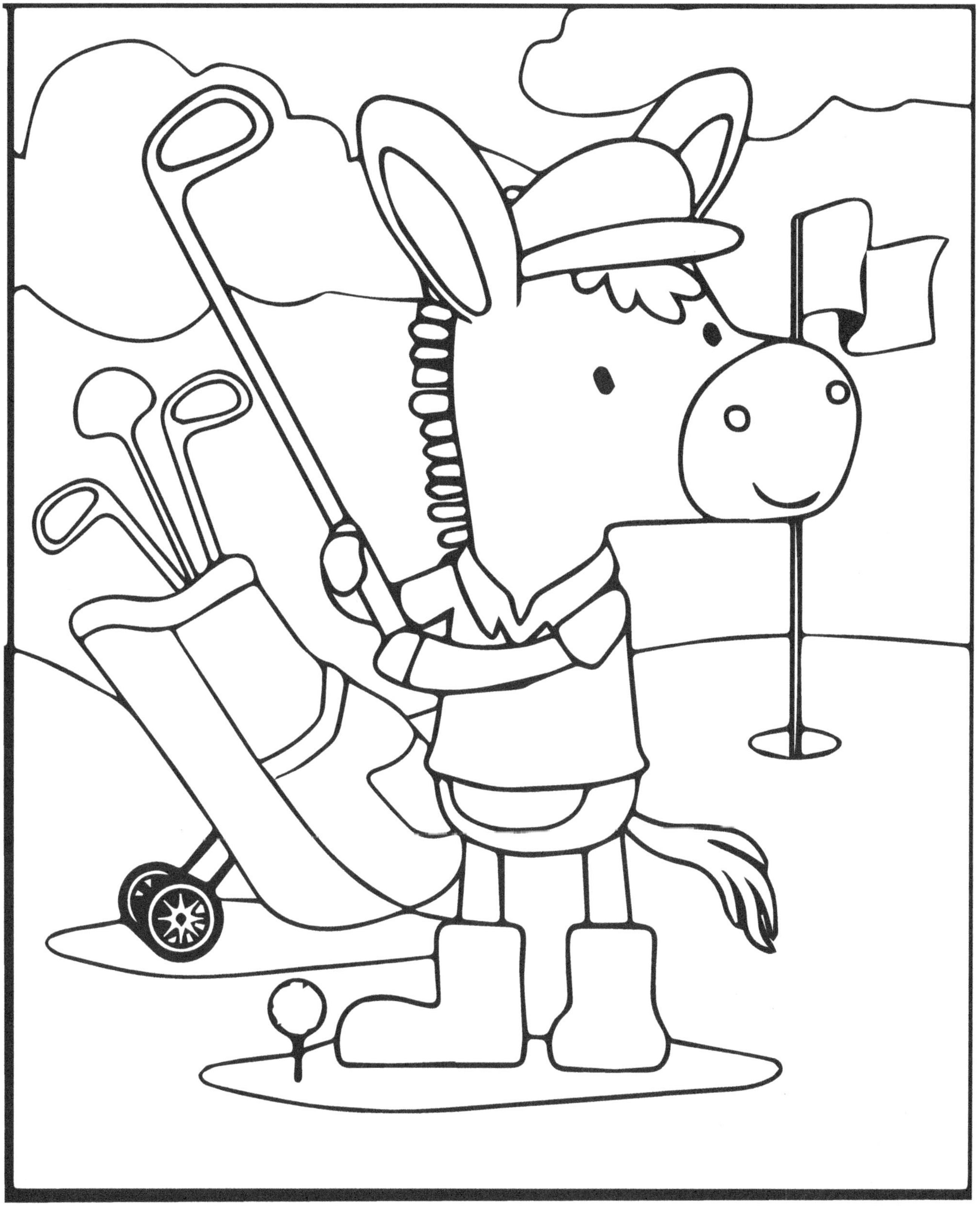

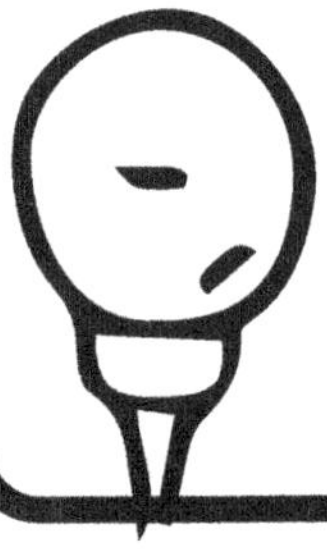

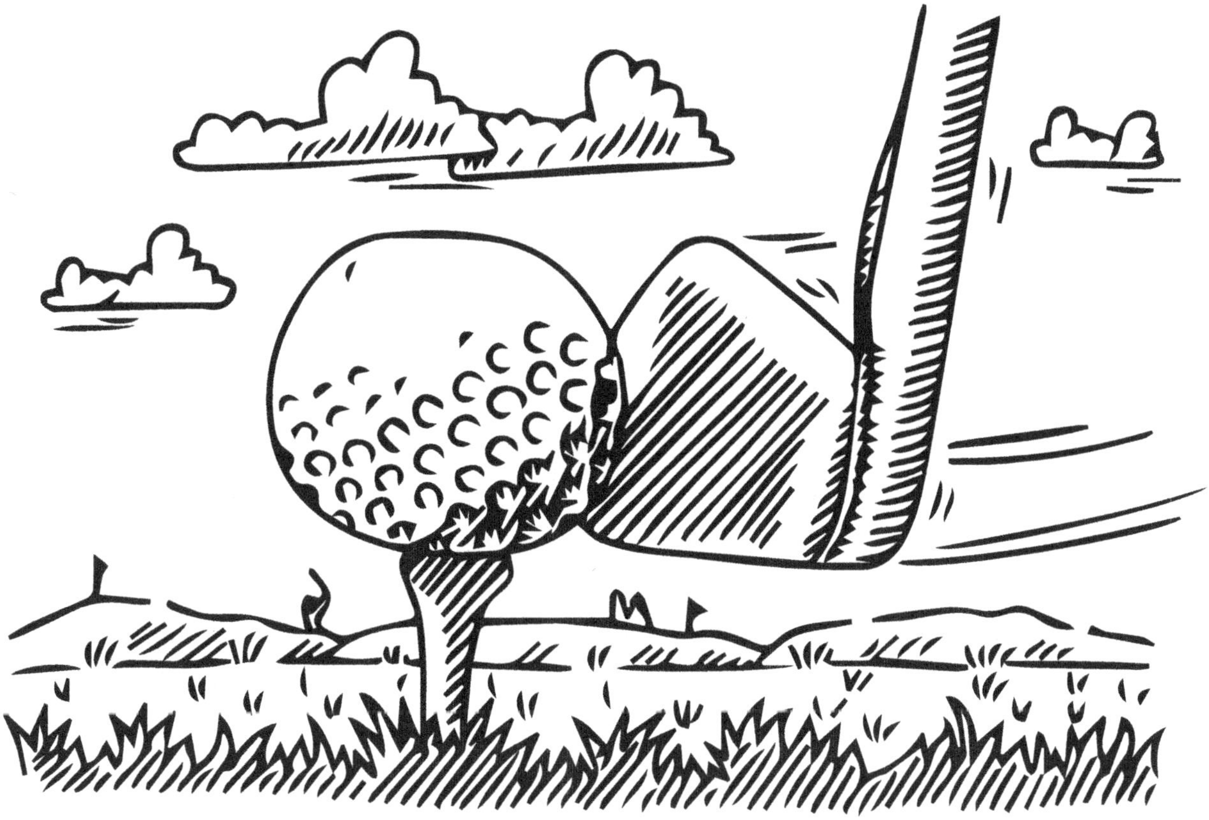

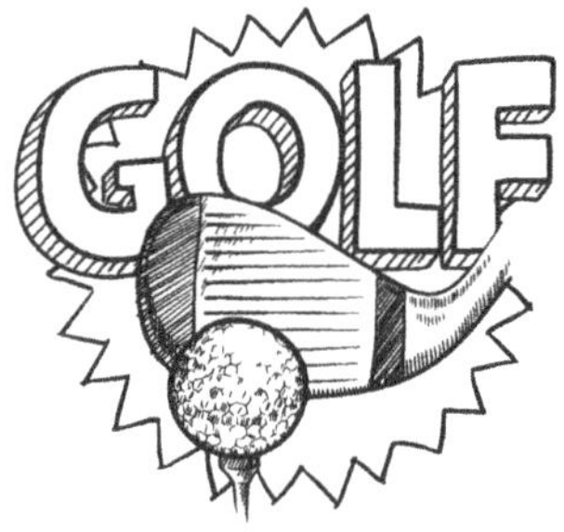
GOLF

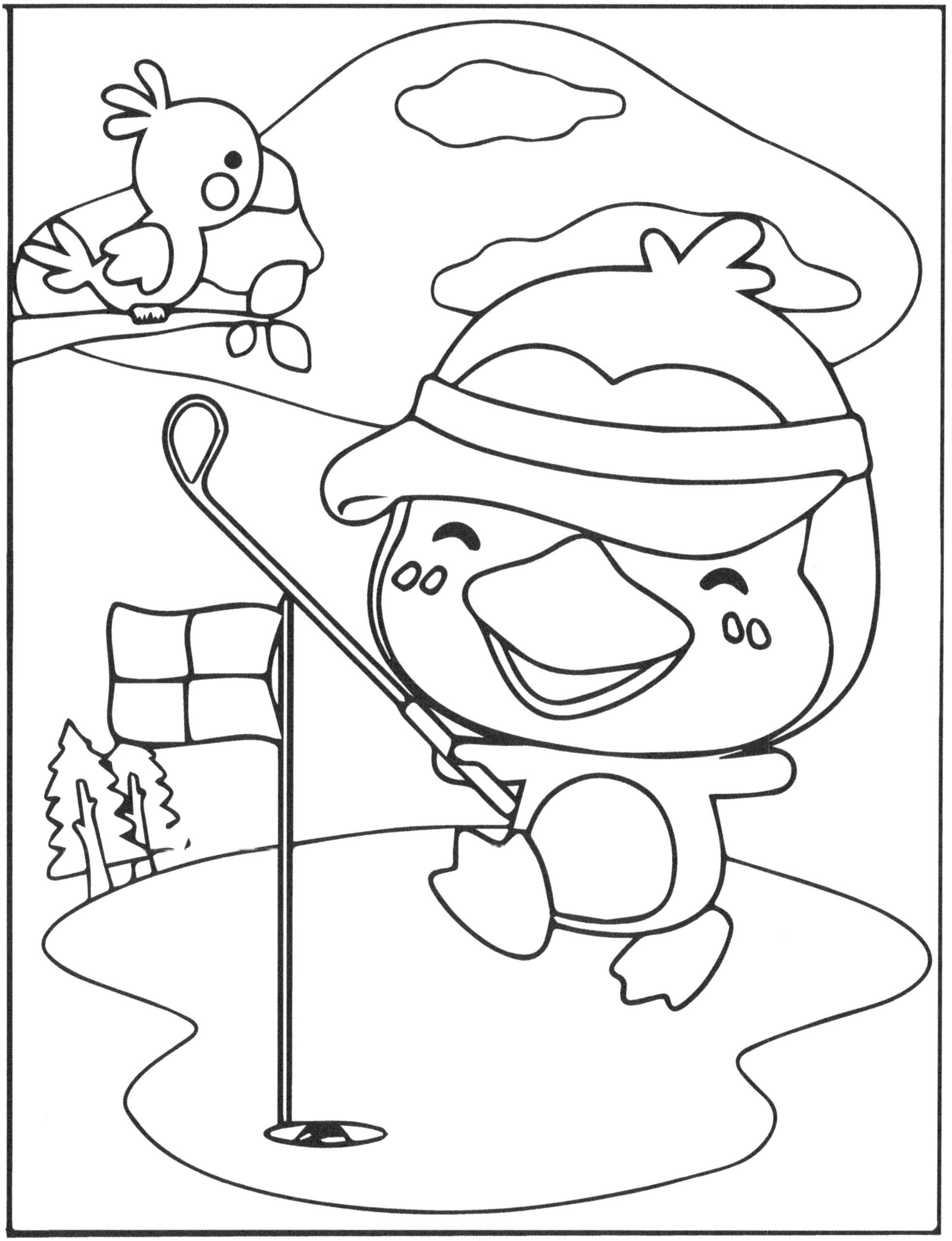

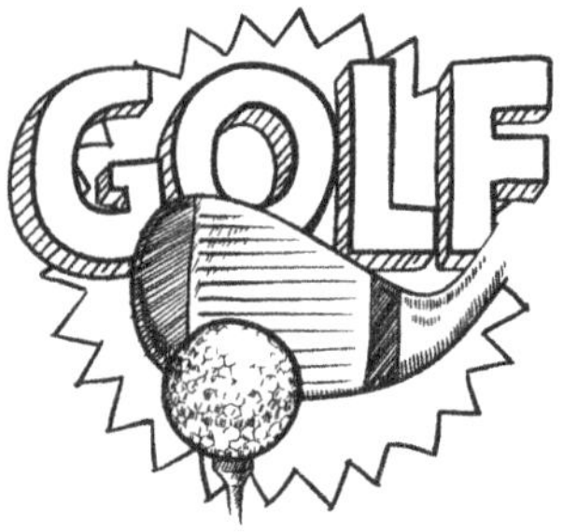
GOLF

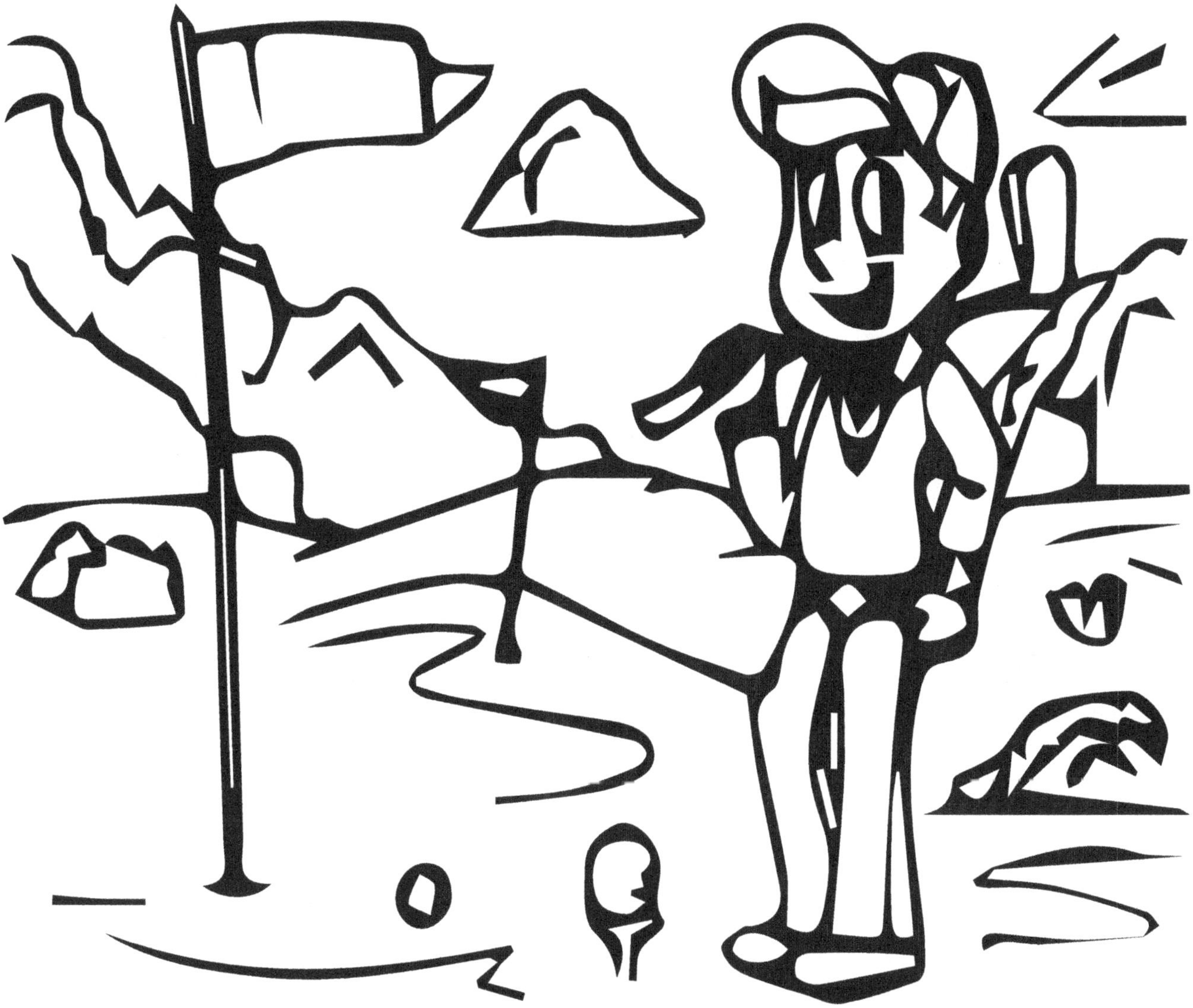

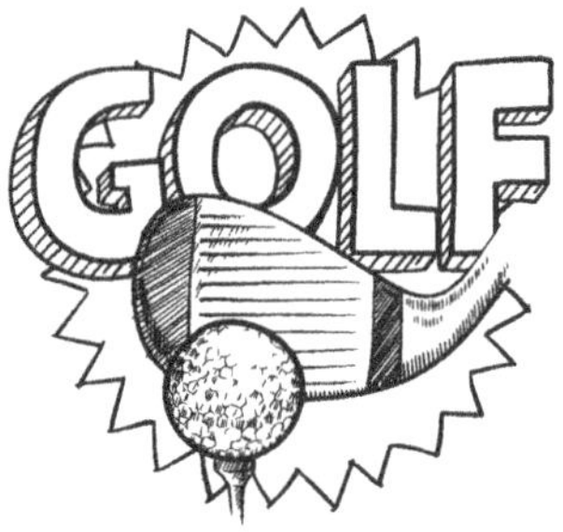
GOLF

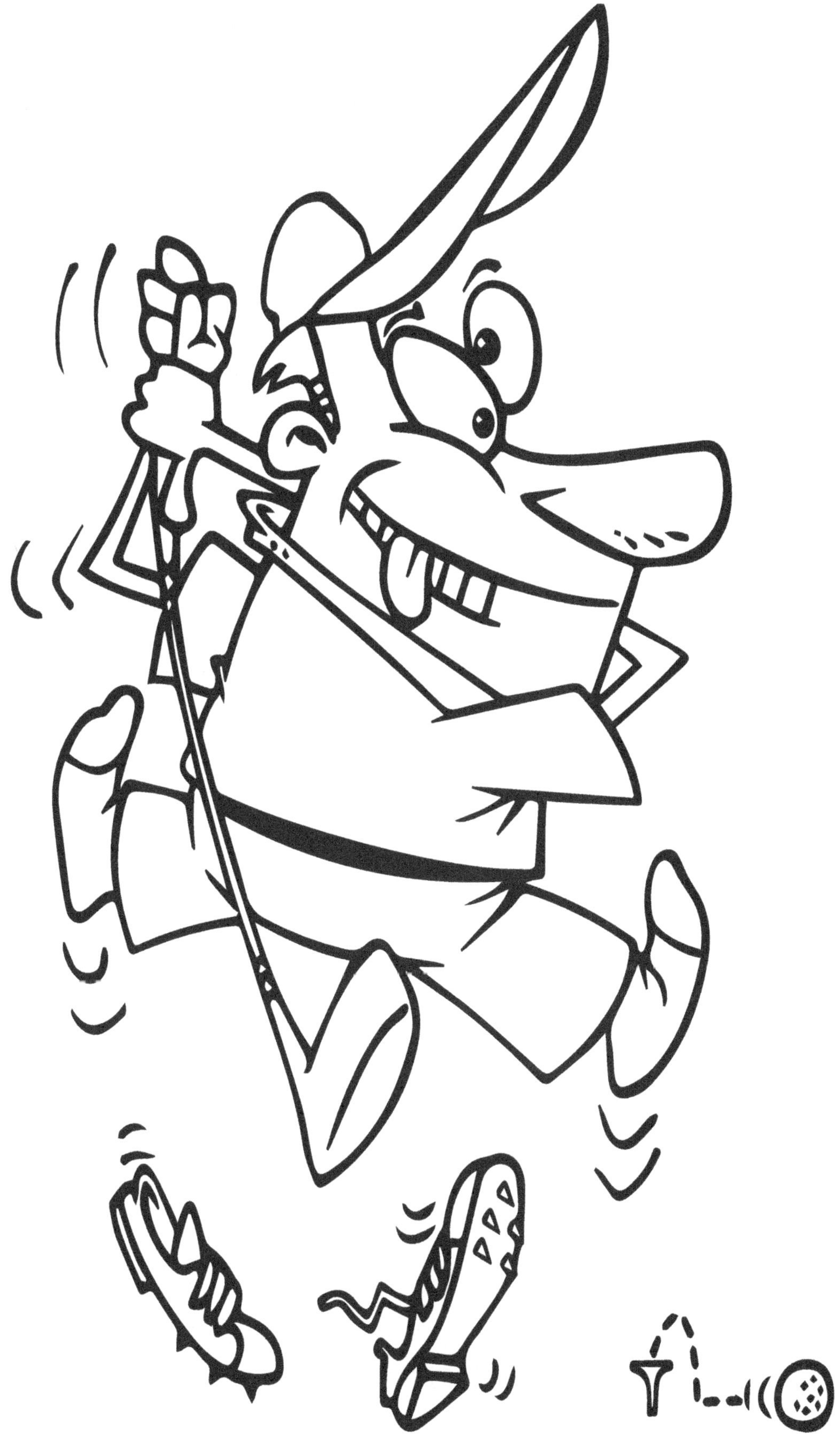

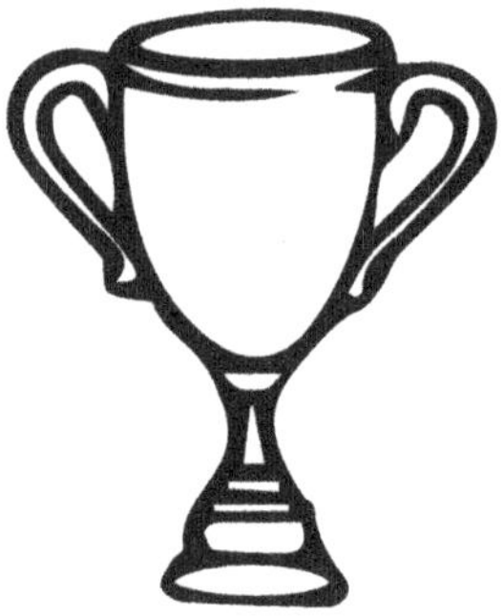

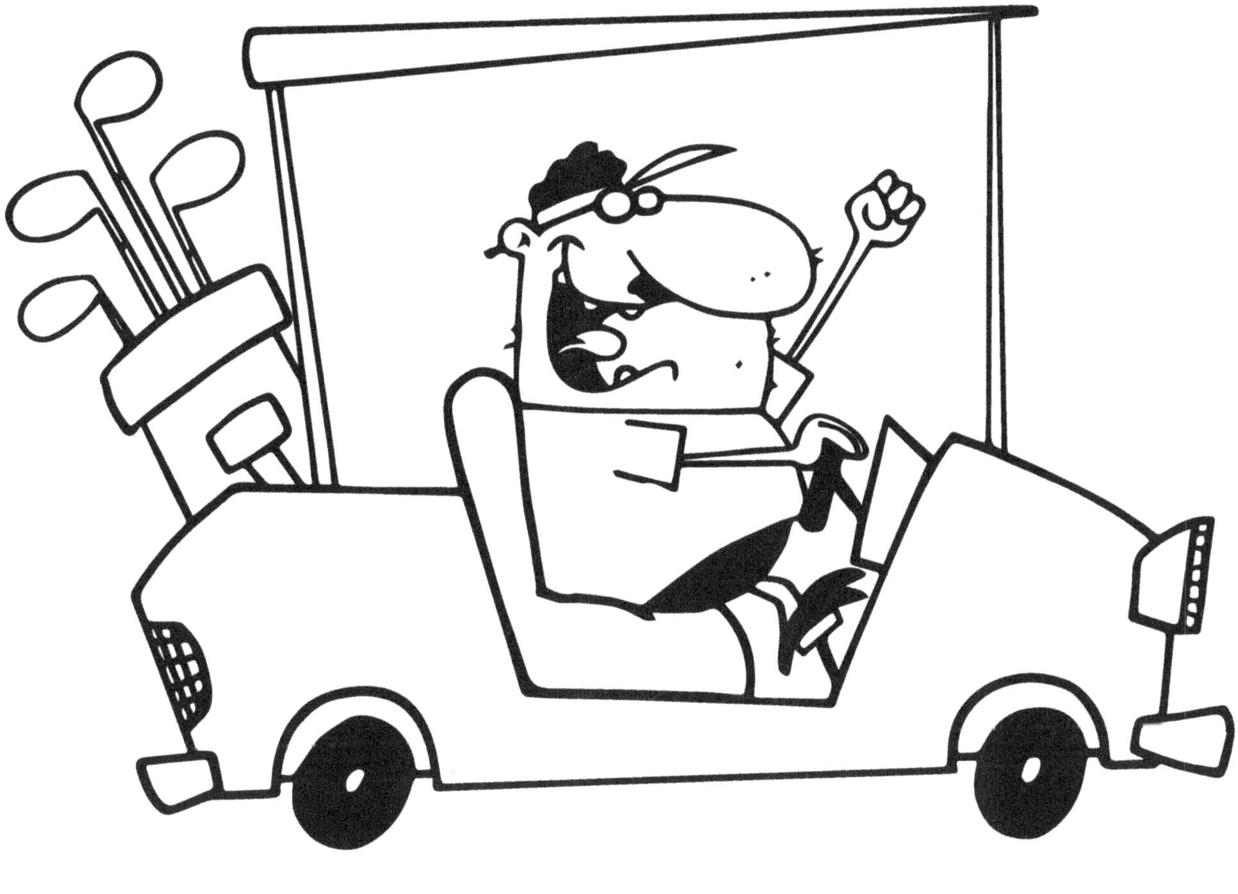

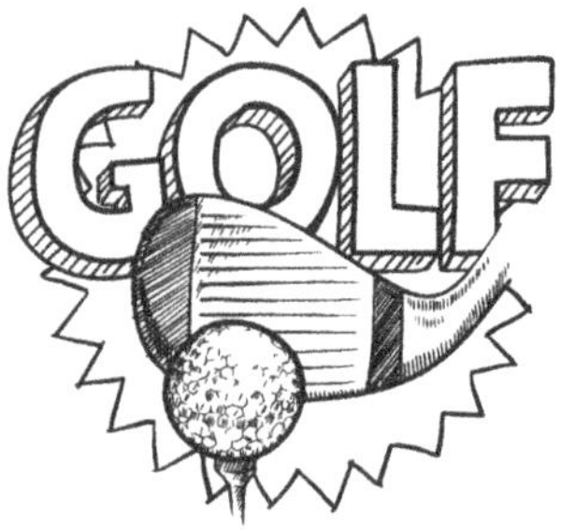
GOLF

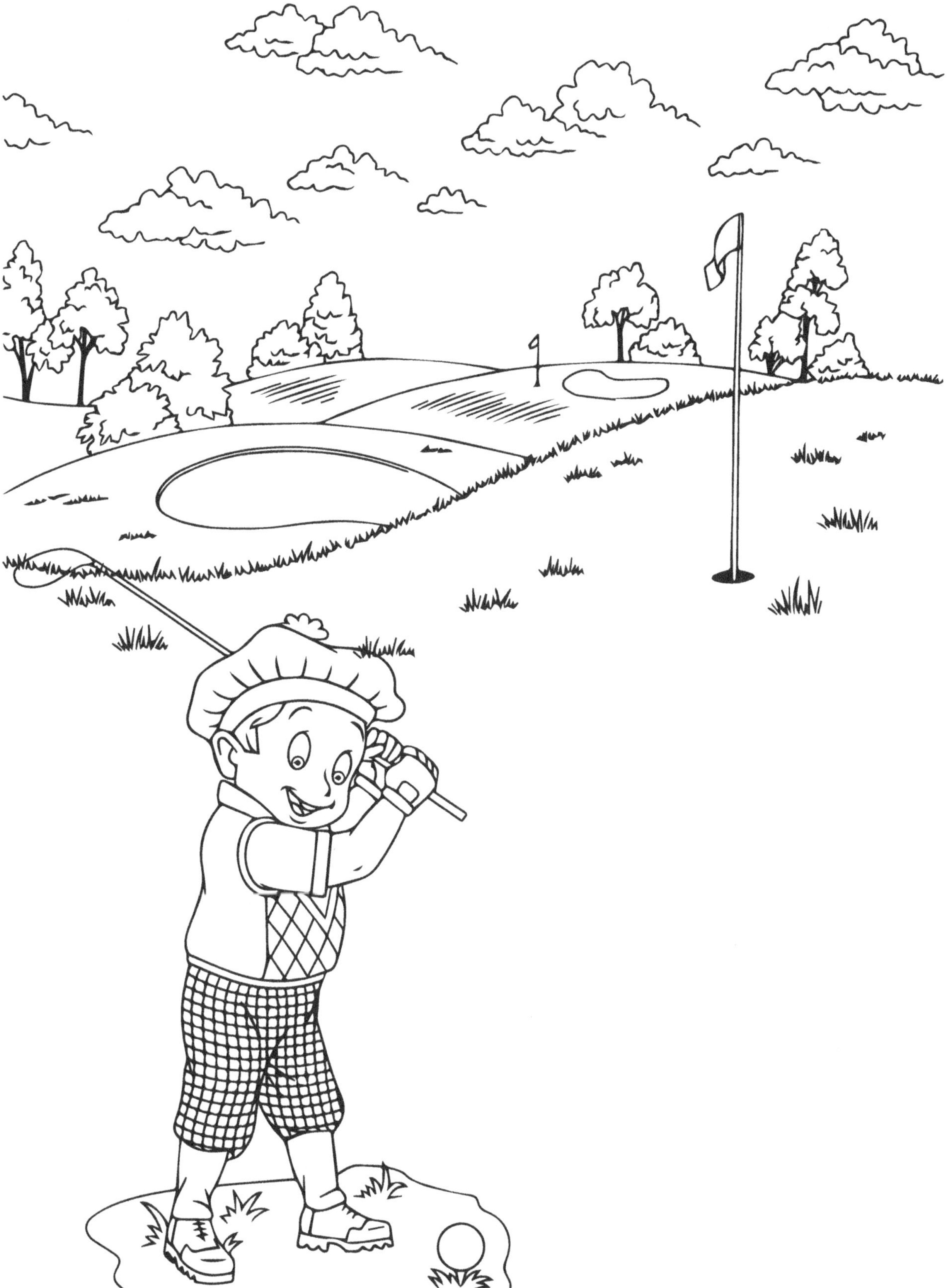

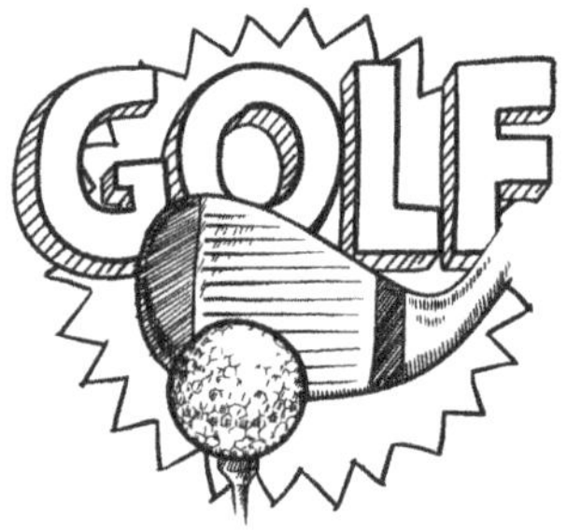
GOLF

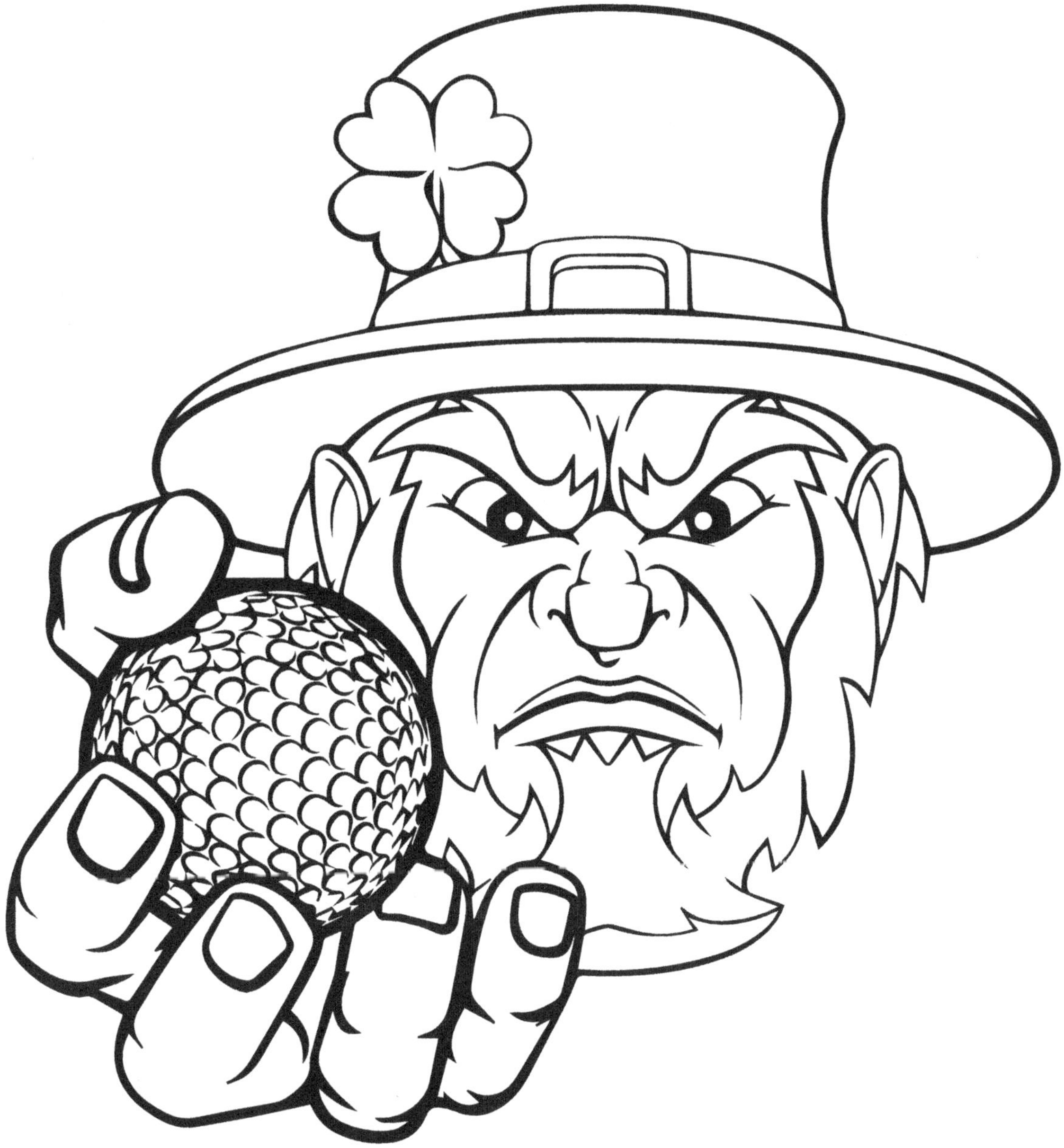

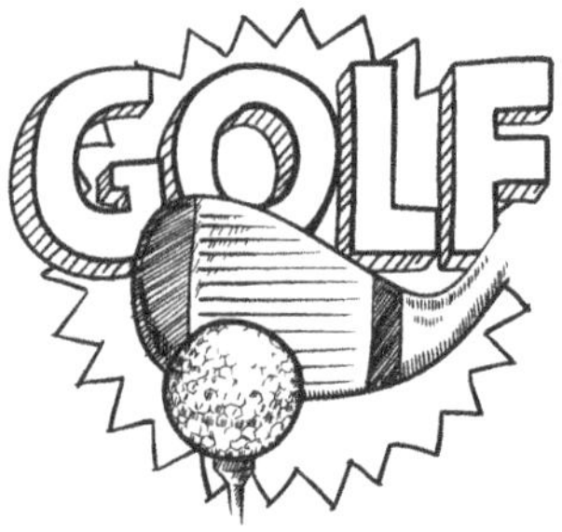
GOLF

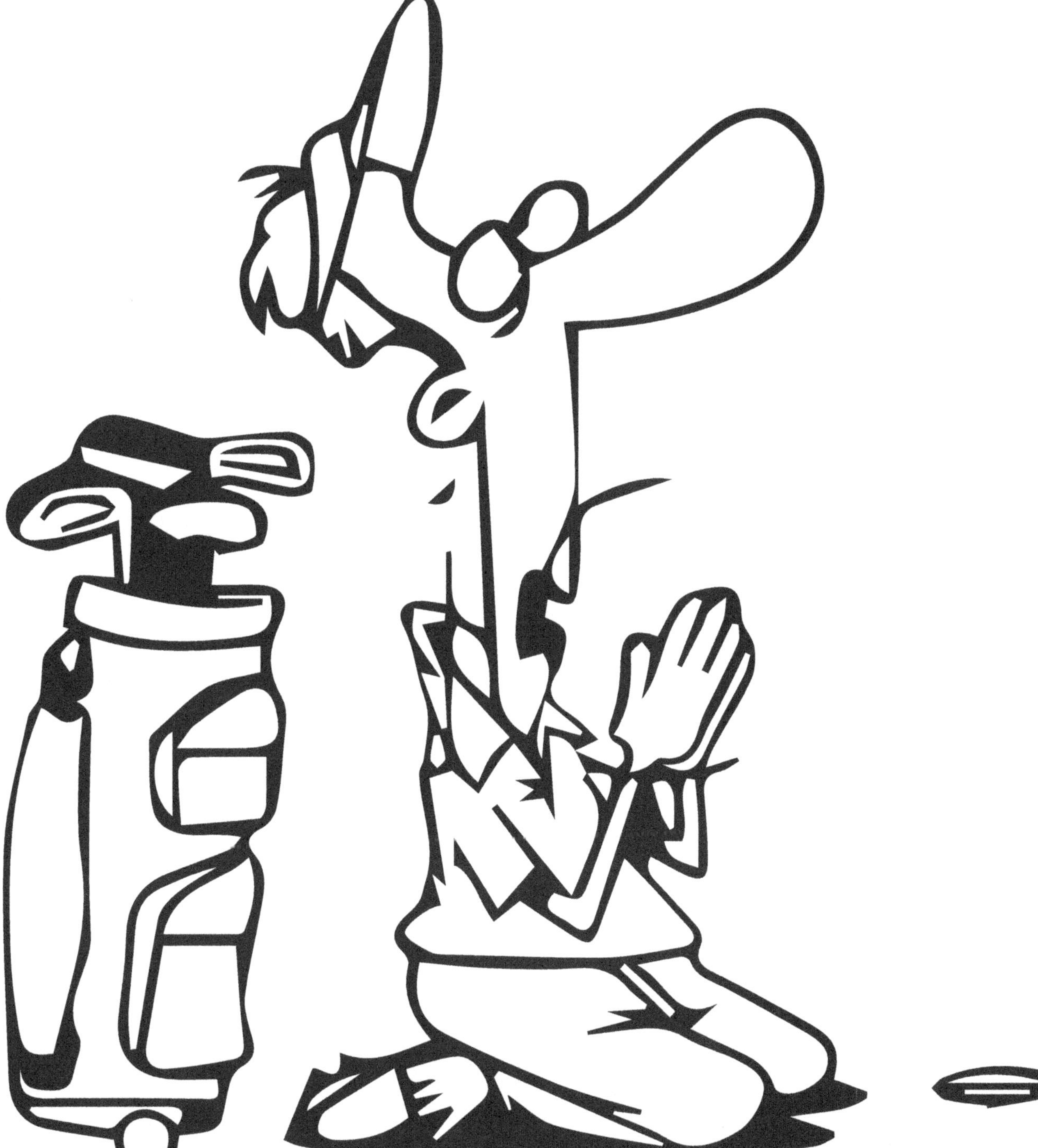

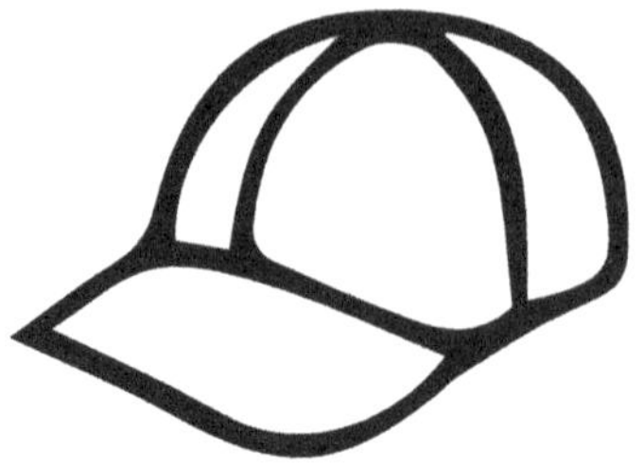

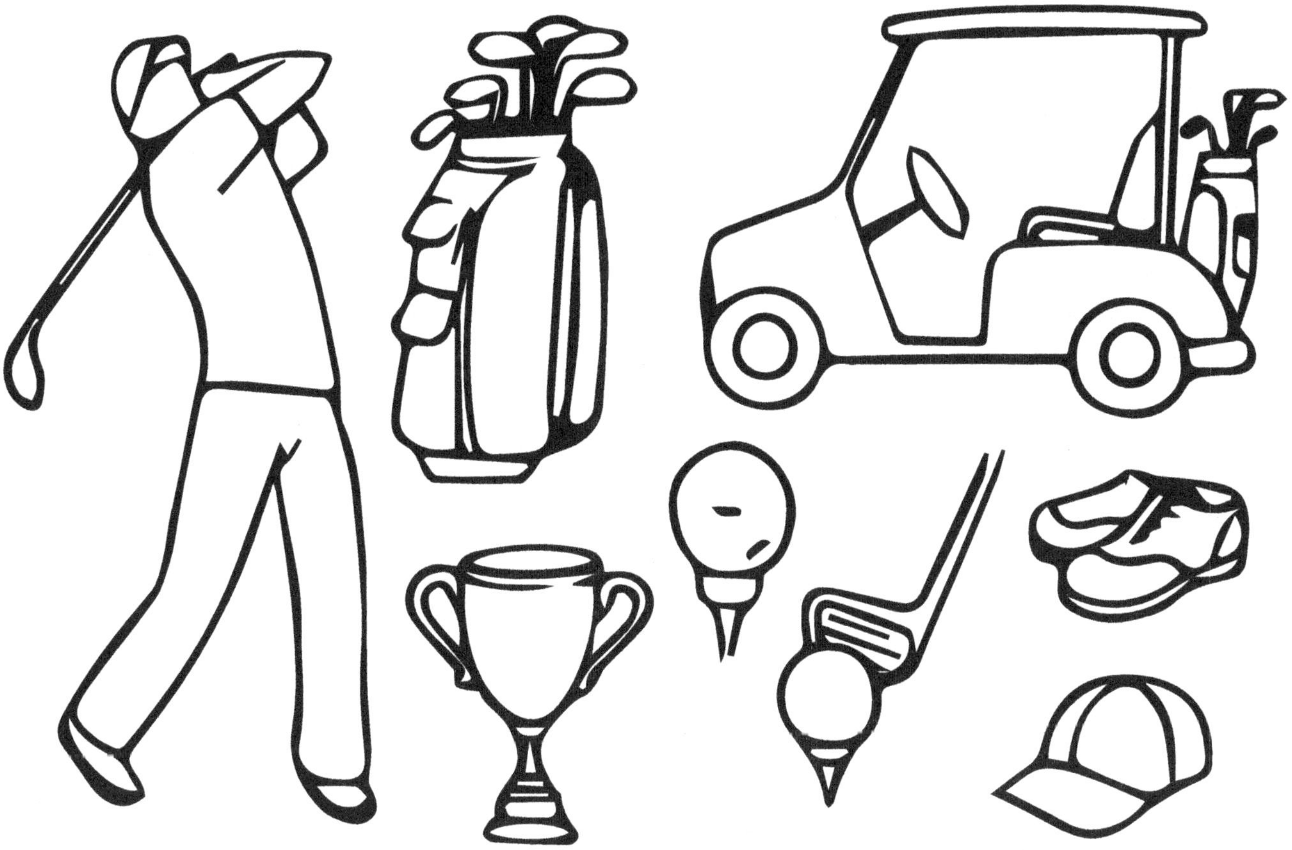

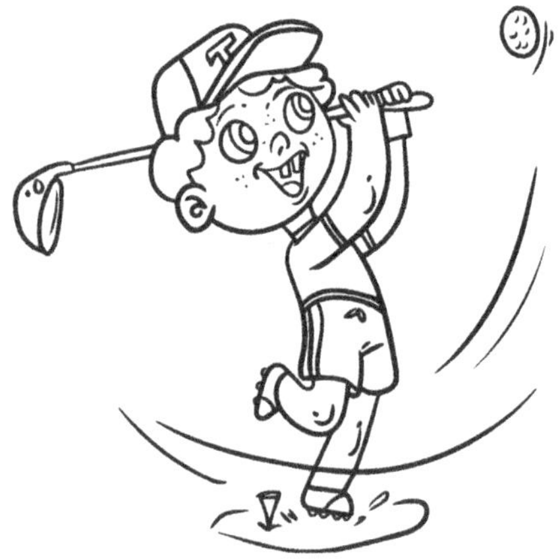

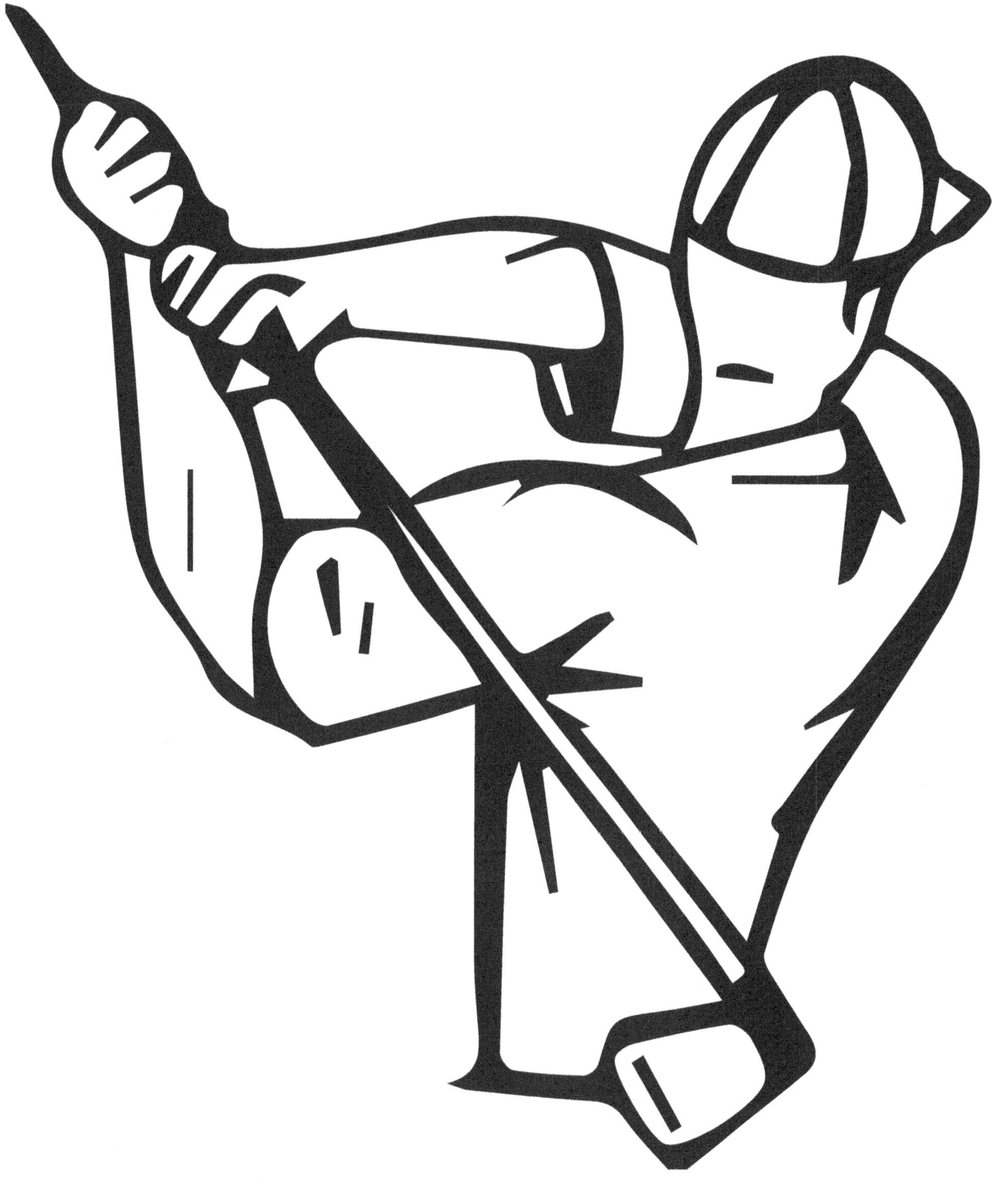

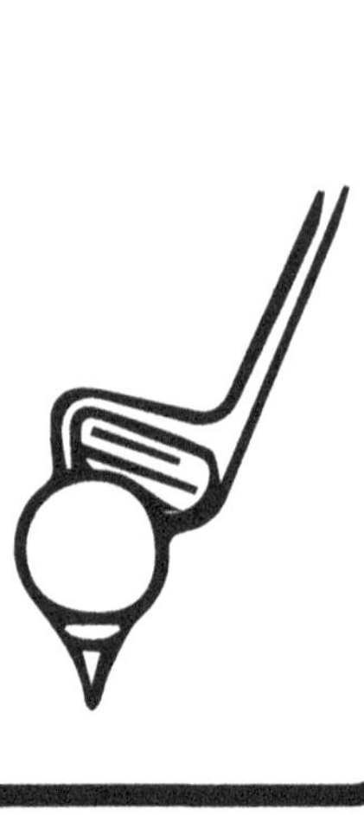

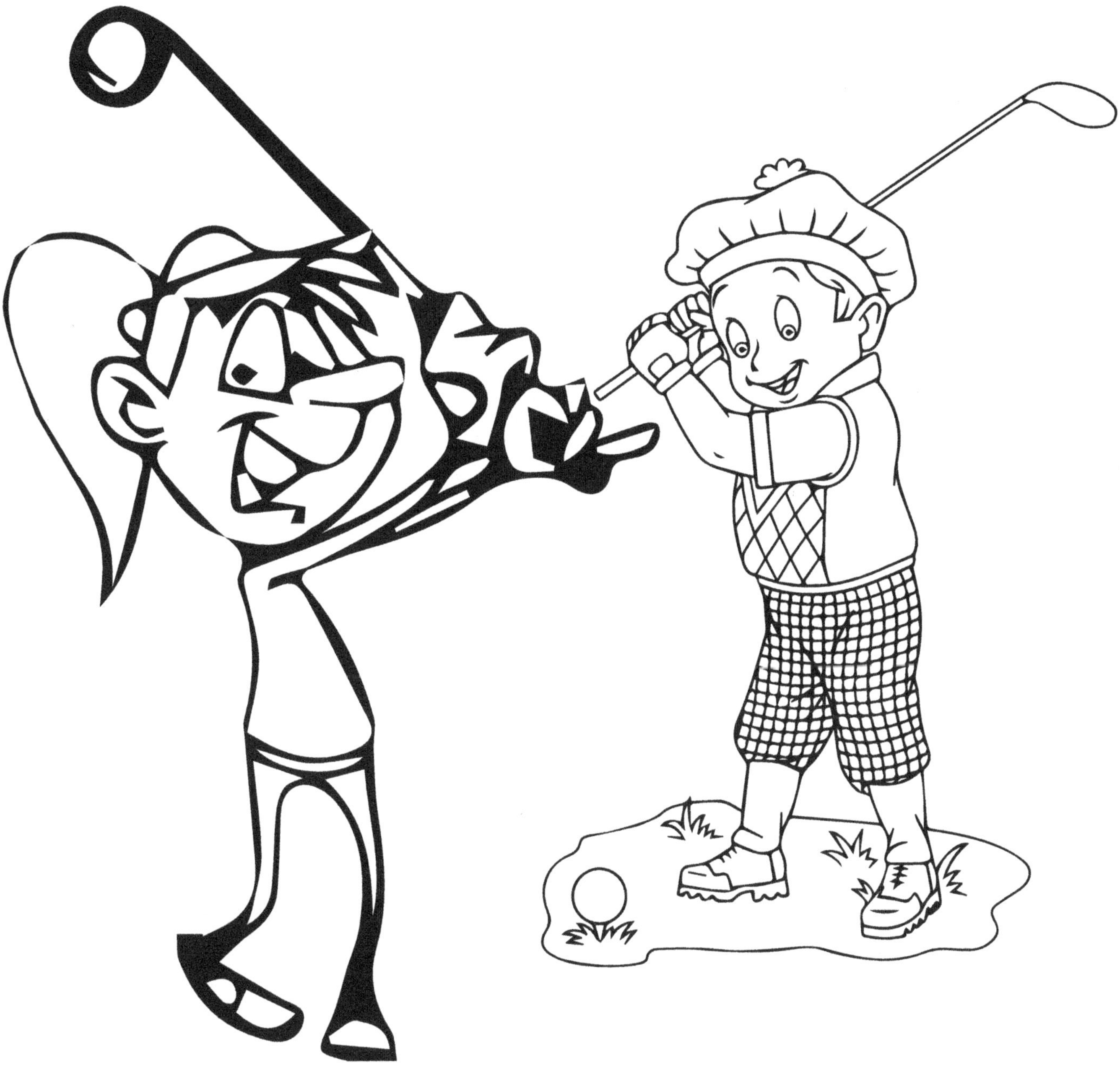

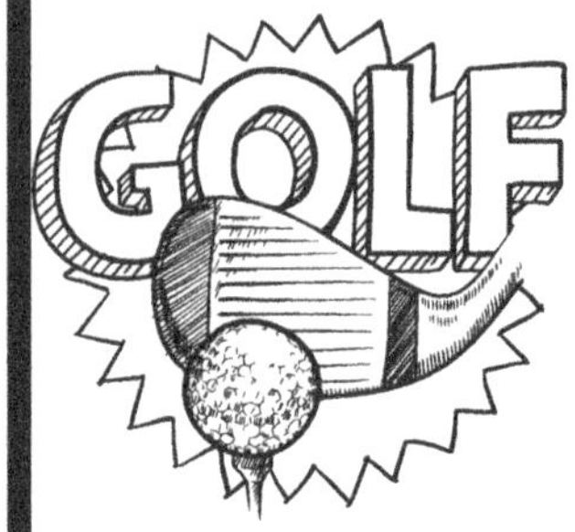
GOLF

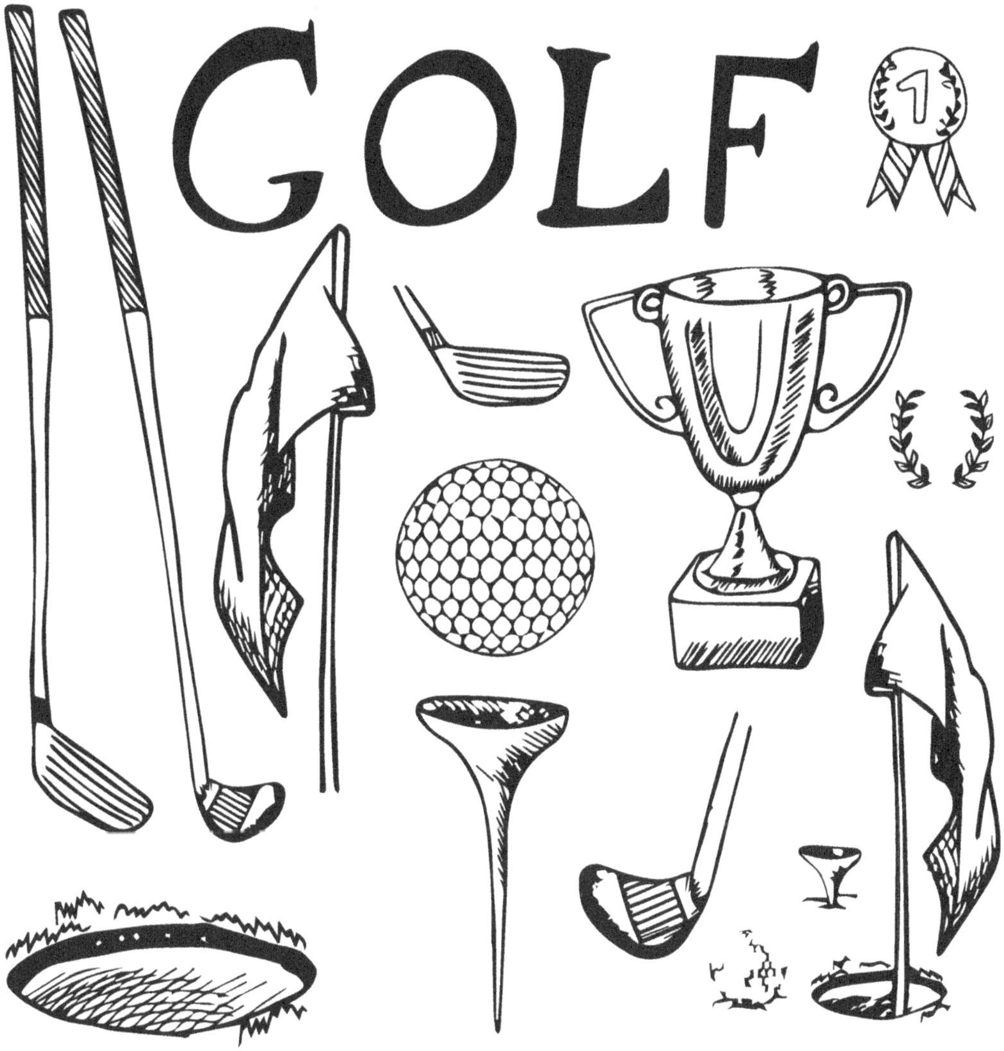
GOLF
1

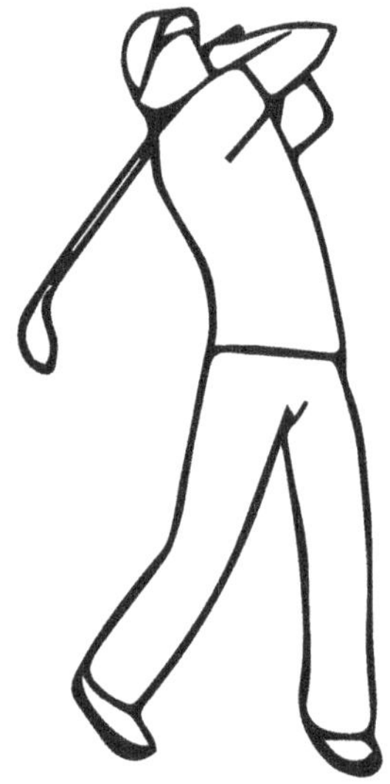

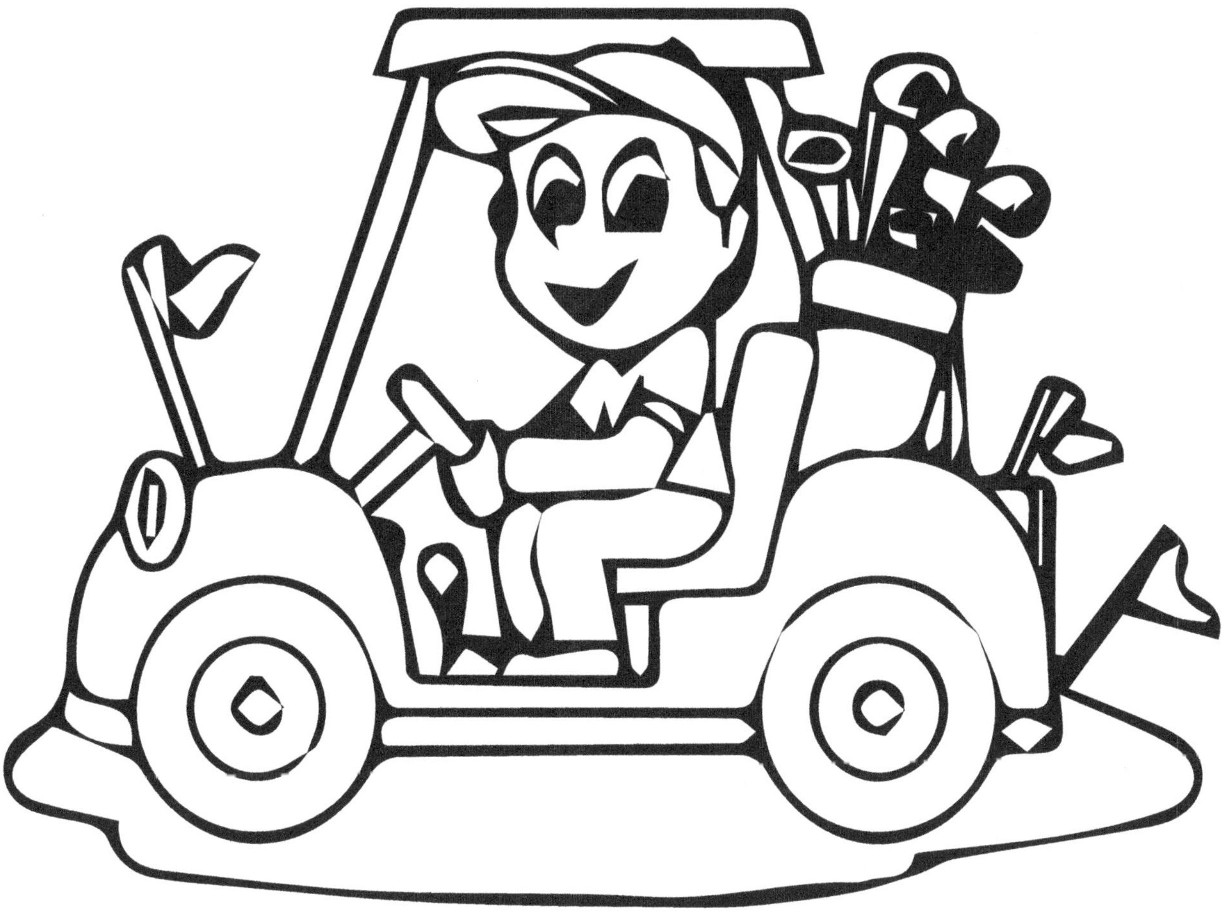

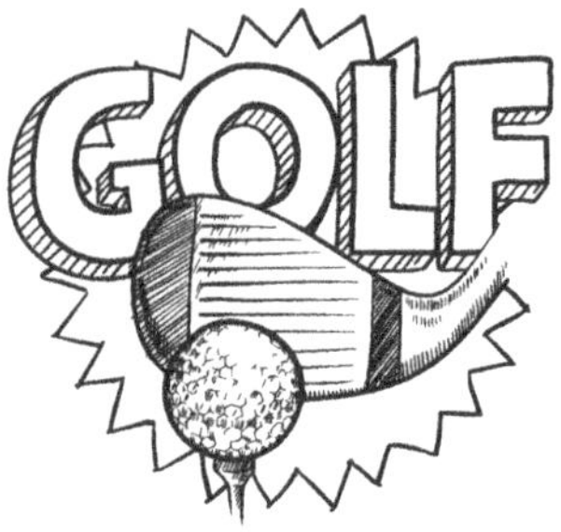
GOLF

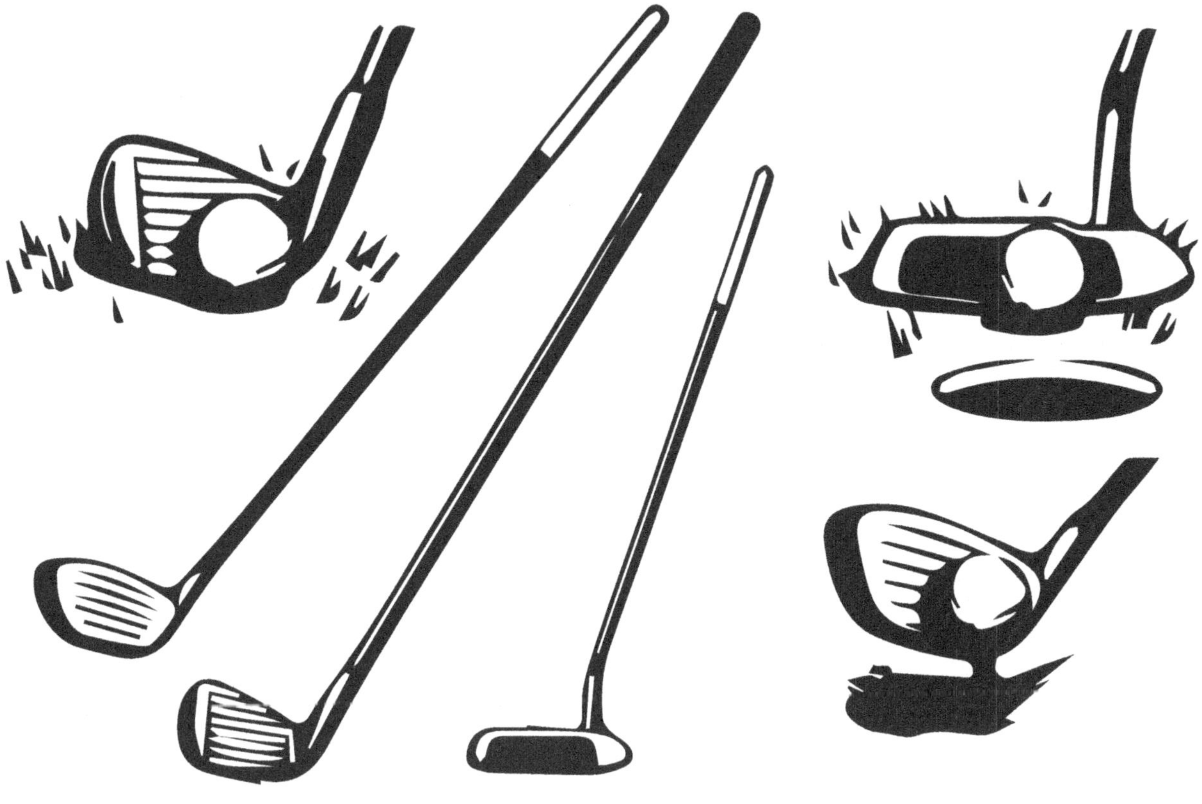

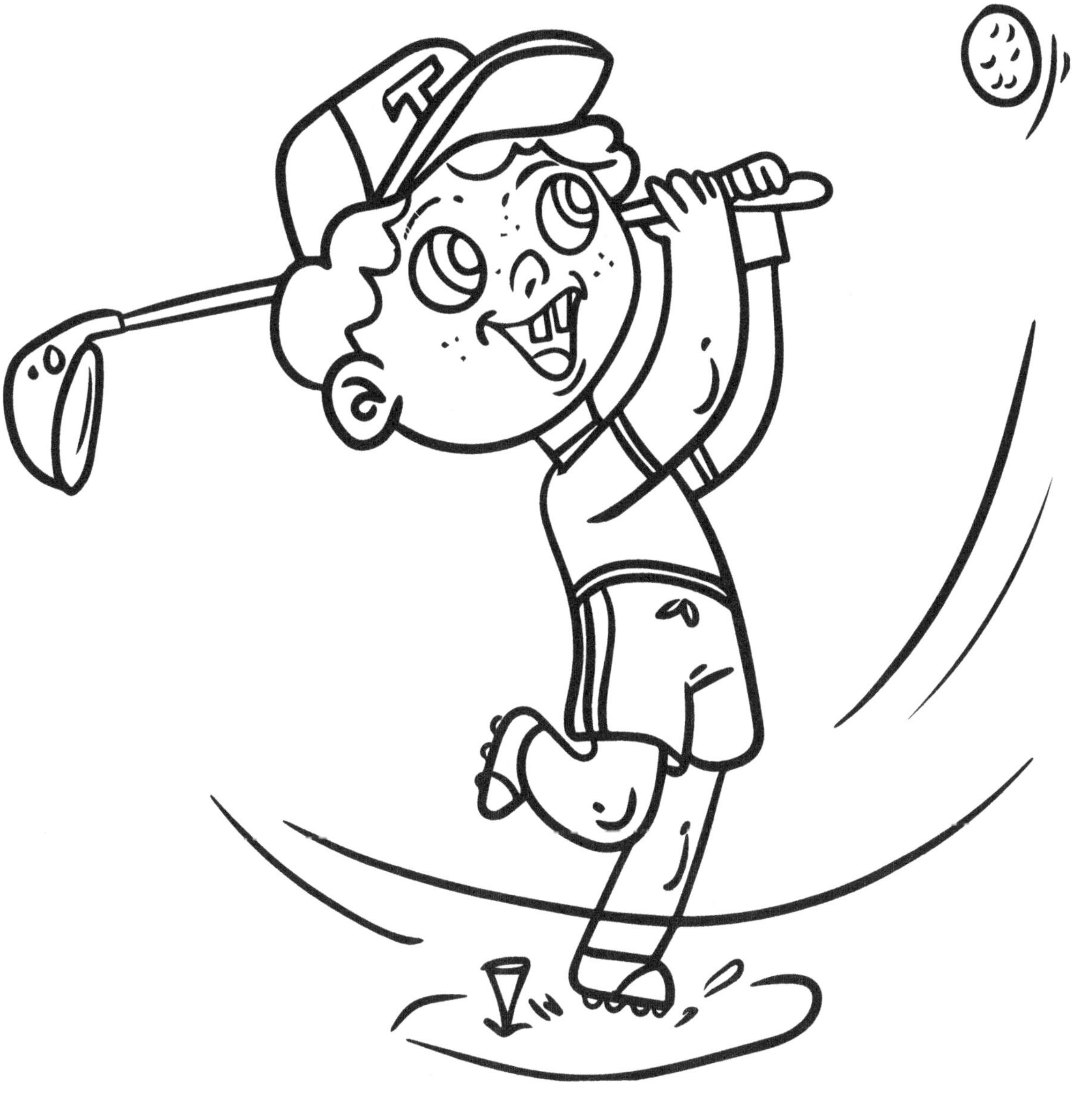

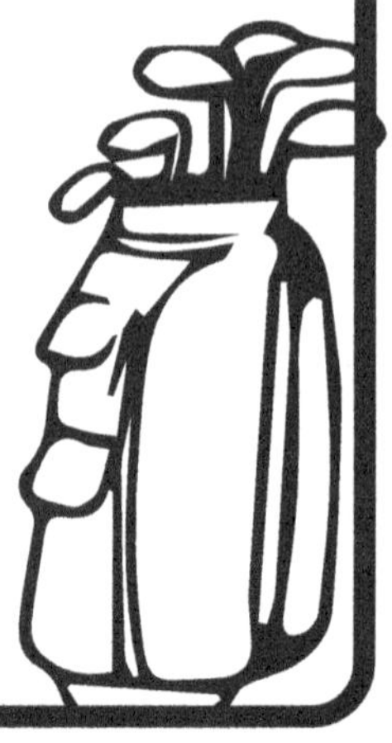

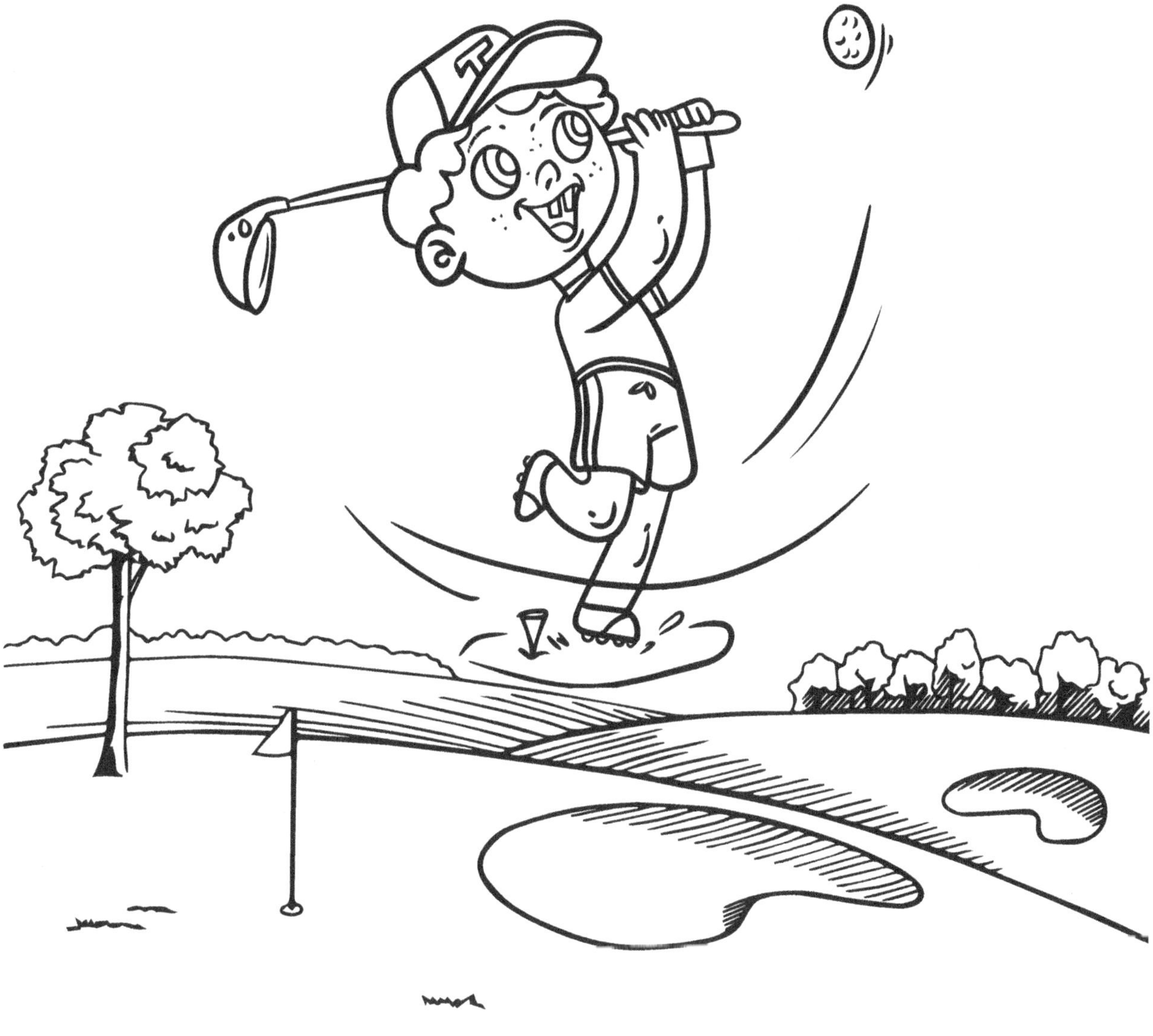

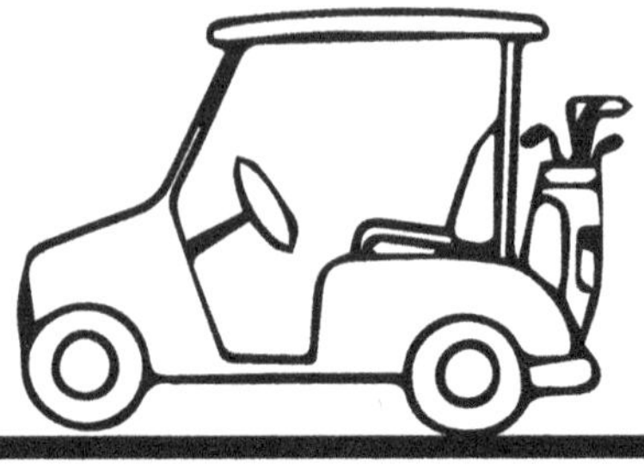

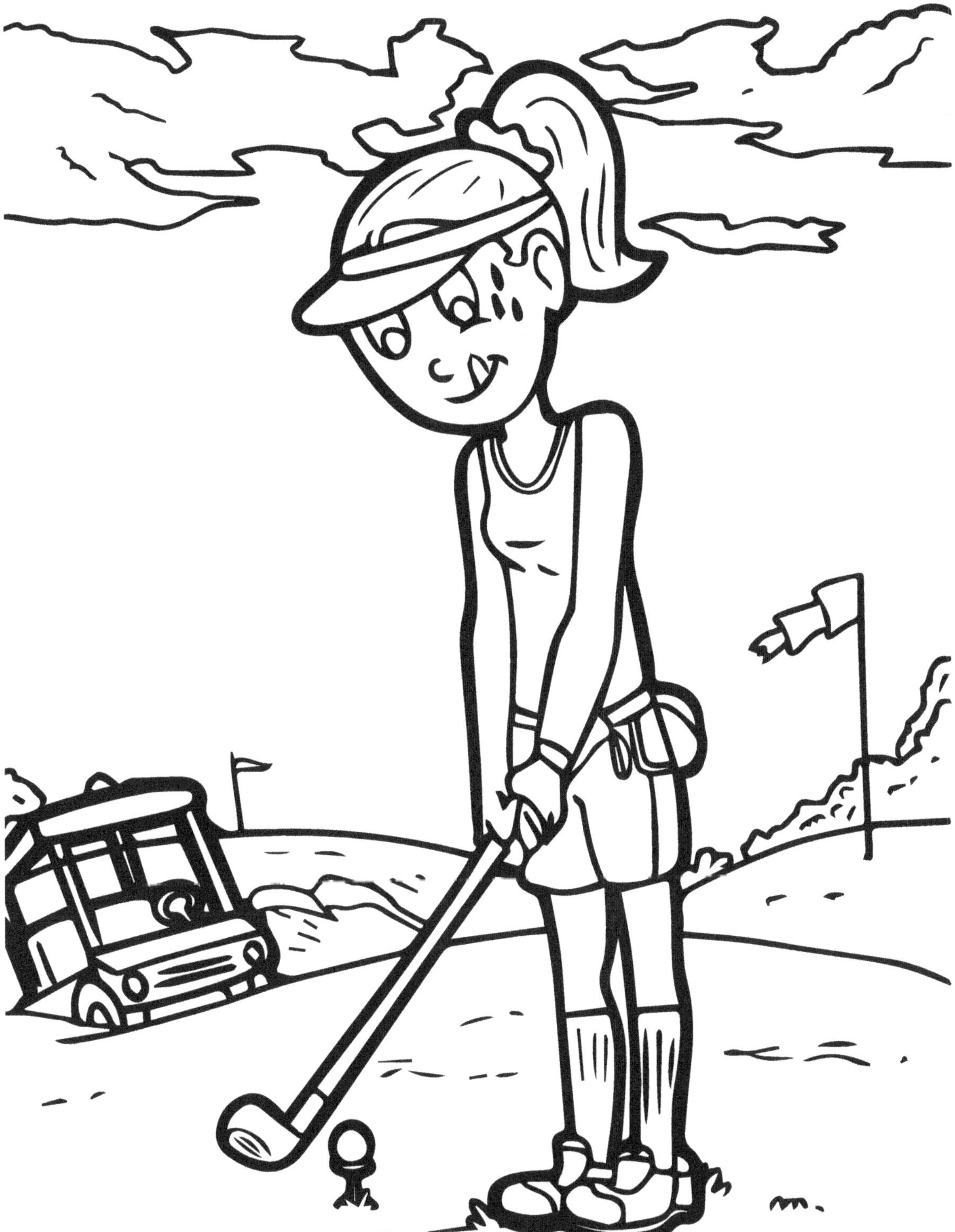

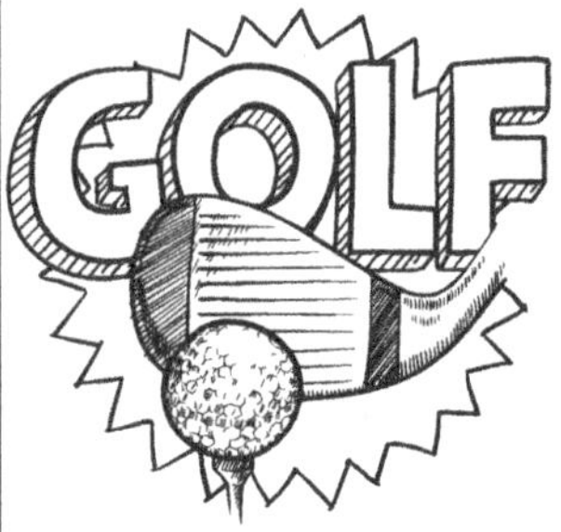
GOLF

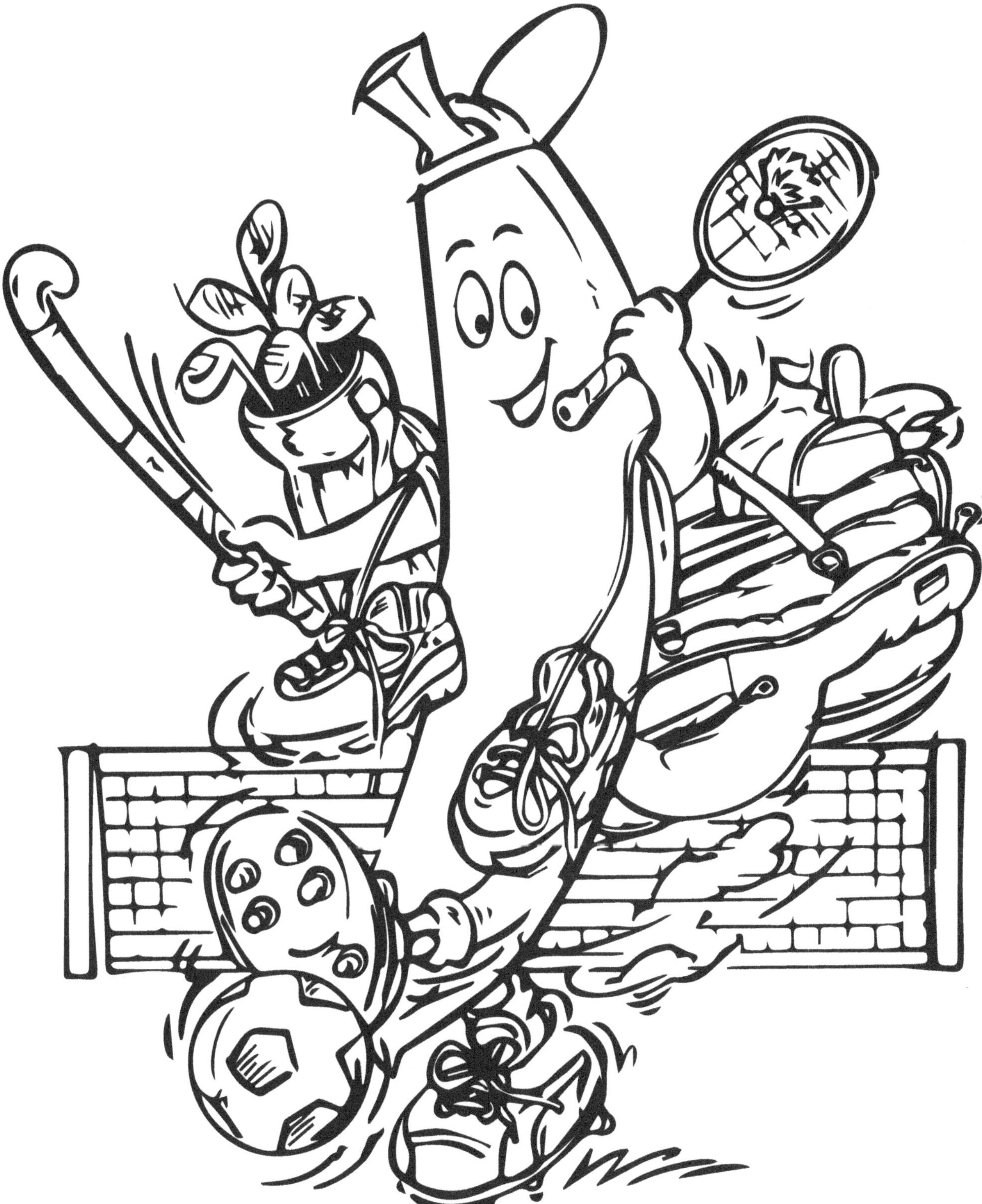

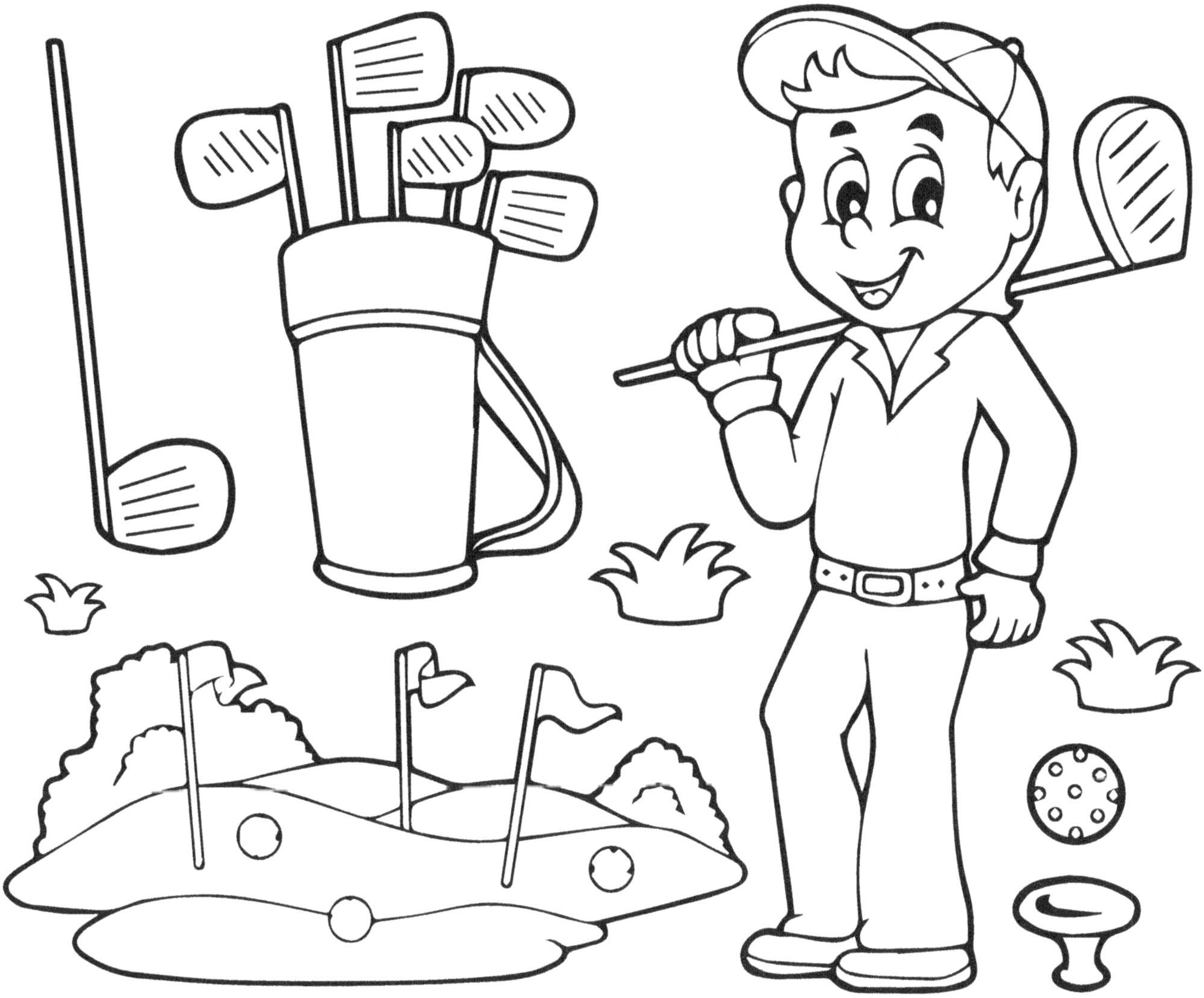

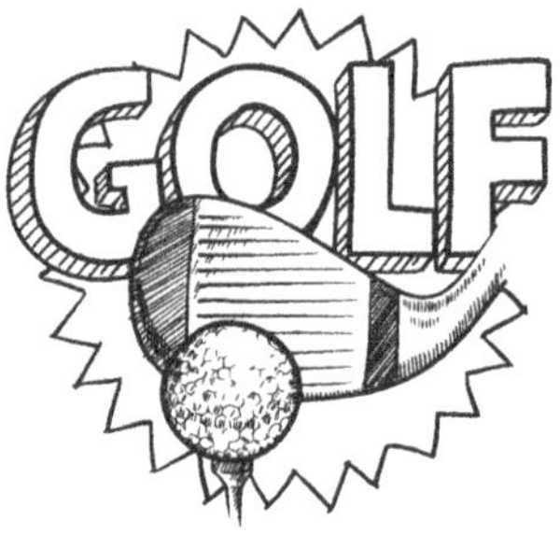
GOLF

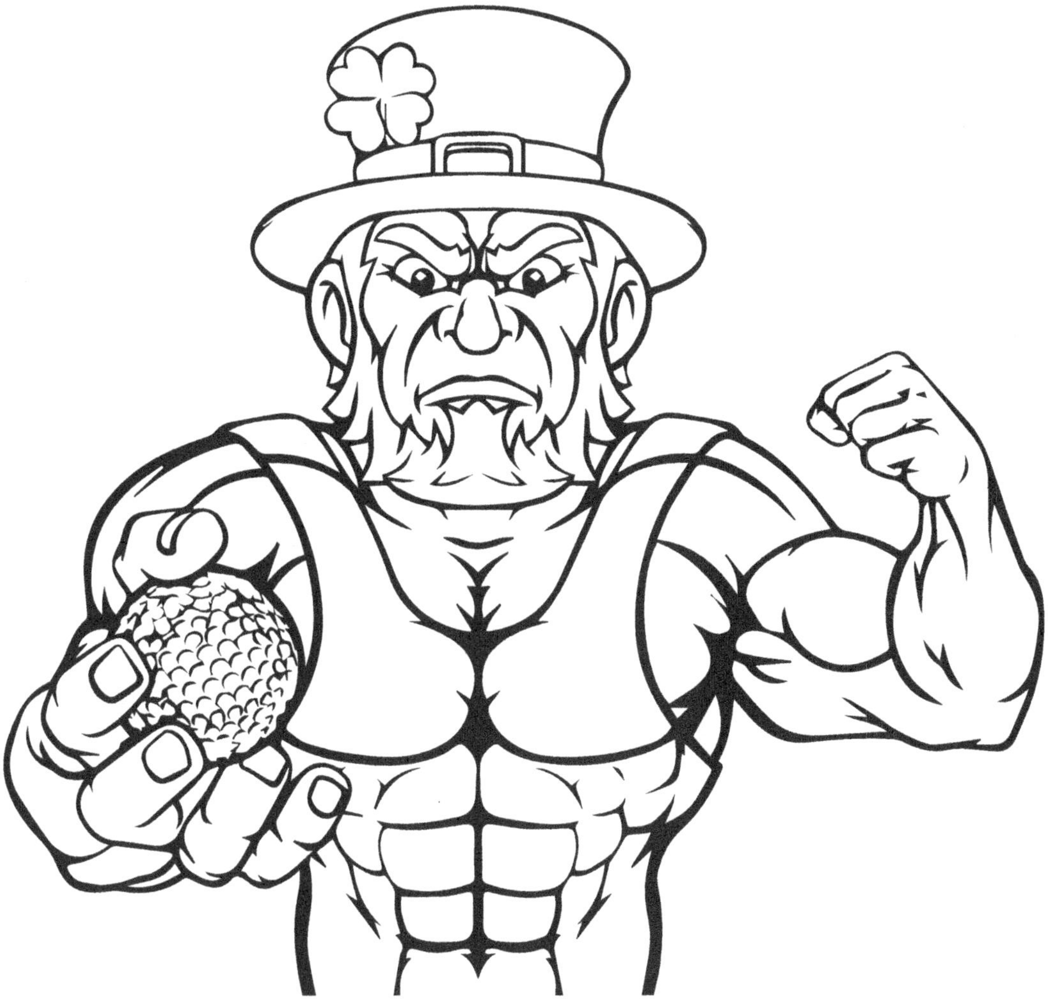

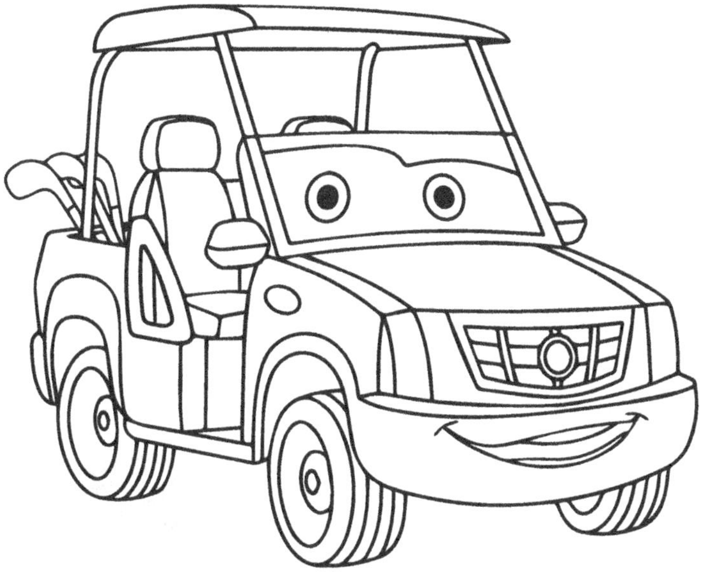

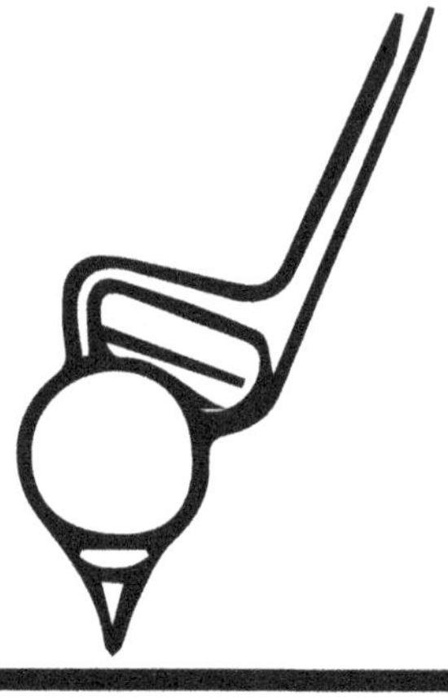

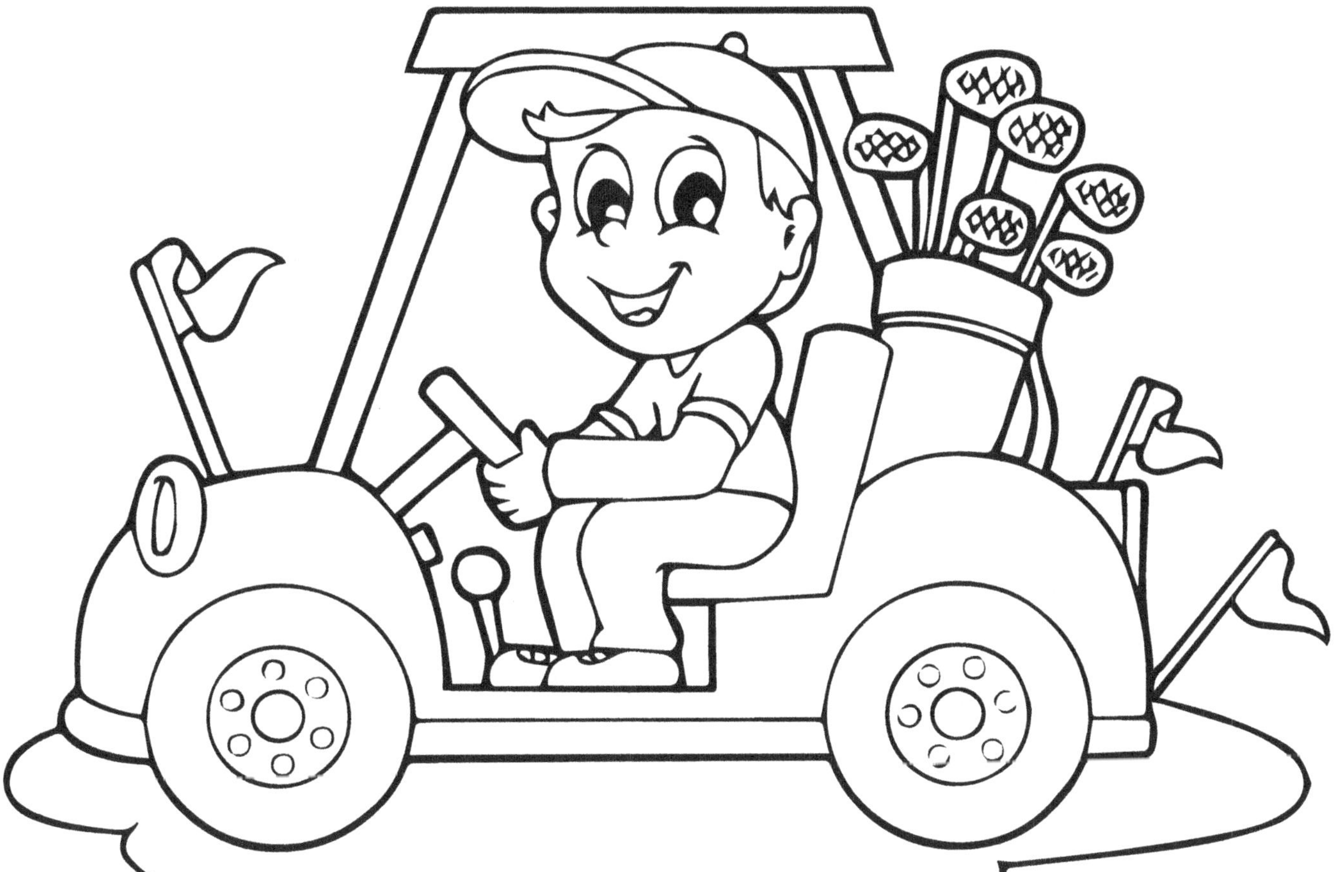

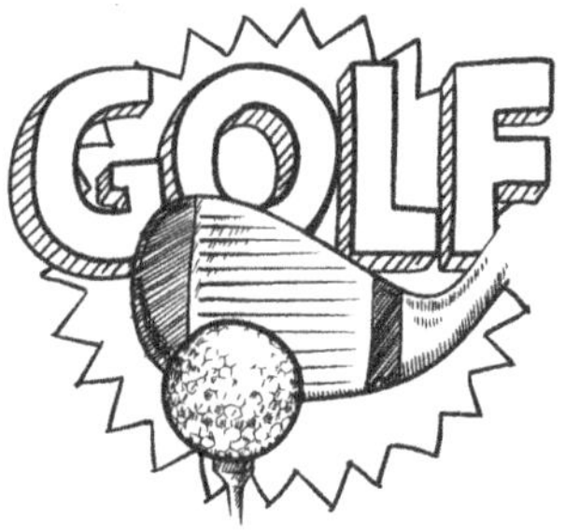
GOLF

Made in the USA
Coppell, TX
27 November 2024

41080497R00031